of the

University of Virginia

1956-57

BAYONET

ALMA MATER

All Hail, dear Alma Mater,
We sing our praise to you,
High on Marye's Hilltop
You stand forever true;
Born in truth and honor
You ever more shall be,
The model of our future years,
And all eternity.
When e'er we have to leave you
We never will forget,
The lessons you have taught us,
And all the friends we've met,
And we your loyal daughters
Will hold your name on high,
So here's to Mary Washington
Our love will never die.

THE BAYONET

o

MARY WASHINGTON COLLEGE

of the

UNIVERSITY OF VIRGINIA

o

1956-1957

o

Presented

by

THE STUDENT GOVERNMENT ASSOCIATION

of

MARY WASHINGTON COLLEGE

FREDERICKSBURG, VIRGINIA

Vol. 33   September, 1956

Editorial Staff

Student Committee:

Betty Davies, Chairman

Connie Hook

Jean Harris

Pat Clark

Beth Poteet

Emmy Hepford

Meg Patton

Evelyn Nitti

Sandy Elroy

Patsy Preston

Faculty Committee:

Dr. Burney Lynch Parkinson, Chairman

Dr. Earl G. Insley

Dr. Eileen K. Dodd

MATRICULATION AT MARY WASHING-
TON COLLEGE CONSTITUTES AN EX-
PLICIT PROMISE AND A PLEDGE ON
THE PART OF THE STUDENT AND HER
PARENTS OR GUARDIAN TO FAMIL-
IARIZE THEMSELVES WITH THE RULES
AND REGULATIONS OF THE COLLEGE,
STUDENT GOVERNMENT, AND THE
HONOR SYSTEM, AND TO CONFORM TO
SUCH REGULATIONS AS LONG AS THE
STUDENT REMAINS IN THE INSTITU-
TION.

COLLEGE TRADITIONS

Students at Mary Washington have a heritage of traditions which have developed over a period of years and are characteristic of the Mary Washington way of life.

Mary Washington students are noted for their friendliness. They smile and speak when they meet on campus.

Mary Washington students are noted for appropriate grooming, poise, courtesy, and refinement.

Mary Washington students take a justifiable pride in the beauty of their buildings and campus. They do not cut across the grass in going from building to building.

Mary Washington students respect the College seal, which is set in the floor of the rotunda of the library, and do not step on it.

The Honor System is a hallowed tradition and has been in effect for over a hundred years at the University.

Some traditional activities and their sponsors are:

     Loyalty Night—YWCA, RA and SGA

     Big and Little Sisters—YWCA

     Peanut Week—YWCA

     Religious Emphasis Week—YWCA

Christmas Party—YWCA, RA and SGA

Christmas Decorations Contest—SGA

Devil-Goat Rivalry—RA

Song Contest—SGA

Faculty—Student Day Picnic—YWCA, RA, and SGA

Senior Day—Junior Class

Freshman Dance—RA

Serenades

These traditions, which may be shared as well by a freshman as by the oldest alumna, give a sense of unity to all who attend Mary Washington College and add new richness and meaning to each year.

CALENDAR OF EVENTS

1956-1957

First Semester

September

Sunday, 16th—Dormitories Open
Monday, 17th—Welcome Party for New Students
Tuesday, 18th—Registration of New Students
Wednesday, 19th—Registration of Upper Classmen
Thursday, 20th—Classes Begin
Friday, 21st—"Meet Your Minister Night"
Saturday, 22nd—Reception for New Students
Sunday, 23rd—Big and Little Sister Church Day
Wednesday, 26th—Loyalty Night Convocation
Saturday, 29th—R. A. Freshman Dance

October

Friday, 5th—I. C. A. Open House
Saturday, 6th—Informal Mixer for All Students
Friday, 12th—"Y" Kid Party
Thursday, 18th—Friday, 19th—Inauguration of Chancellor Simpson
Saturday, 20th—"Y" Benefit

November

Saturday, 10th—Senior-Junior Semi-Formal Dance
Wednesday, 14th-Tuesday, 20th—Peanut Week
Saturday, 17th—Freshman Semi-Formal Dance
Wednesday, 21st—Thanksgiving Holidays Begin at
   12:30 P. M.
Monday, 26th—Classes Resumed at 8:30 A.M.

December

    Saturday, 1st—Christmas Formal Dance
    Saturday, 8th—"Y" Toy Show
    Saturday, 8th—Senior Benefit
    Thursday, 13th—S. G. A. Christmas Party
    Saturday, 15th—Christmas Holidays Begin at 12:30
        P. M.

January

    Thursday, 3rd—Classes Resumed at 8:30 A.M.
    Friday, 11th—R. A. Benefit
    Saturday, 19th—Sophomore Semi-Formal Dance
    Thursday, 24th—Reading Day (Closed Day)
    Friday, 25th—Examinations Begin

Second Semester

February

    Monday, 4th—Classes Resumed at 8:30 A.M.
    Wednesday, 6th-Sunday, 10th—Religious Emphasis
        Week
    Saturday, 16th—Junior Benefit
    Wednesday, 27—Song Contest

March

    Saturday, 2nd—Freshman Semi-Formal Dance
    Saturday, 16th—Emerald Ball
    Saturday, 23rd—Sophomore Benefit
    Saturday, 30th—Sophomore Semi-Formal Dance

April

    Friday, 5th-Sunday, 7th—Alumnae Week End
    Saturday, 13th—Junior Ring Dance
    Thursday, 18th—Spring Holidays Begin at 12:30
        P. M.

Wednesday, 24th—Classes Resumed at 8:30 A. M.
Saturday, 27th—Freshman Benefit

May

Saturday, 4th—May Day—May Day Dance
Friday, 24th—Reading Day (Closed Day)
Saturday, 25th—Examinations Begin
Friday, 31st—Senior Benefit

June

Saturday, 1st—Senior Class Day
Sunday, 2nd—Baccalaureate Sermon
Monday, 3rd—Graduation Exercises

OFFICE HOURS AND SERVICES

I. George Washington Office Hours

The Chancellor, the Dean of the College, the Dean of
Women, the Bursar, the Registrar, the Director of Public
Relations, Placement Director, and Director of Admissions:

Monday through Friday:
9:00 a.m.—1:00 p.m.
2:00 p.m.—5:00 p.m.
Saturday:
9:00 a.m.—1:00 p.m.

Students' Bank

Monday through Friday:
9:30 a.m.—12:00 p.m.
2:30 p.m.— 4:00 p.m.
Saturday:
9:30 a.m.—11:30 a.m.

II. E. Lee Trinkle Library:

Monday through Saturday:
    8:00 a.m.—5:45 p.m.
    7:00 p.m.—9:30 p.m.
Sunday:
    2:00 p.m.—5:00 p.m.

III. Dining Hall

Meal hours:
Monday through Saturday:
    Breakfast—7:30 a.m.—8:15 a.m.
    Lunch—1:00 p.m.
    Dinner—6:00 p.m.
Sunday:
    Breakfast—8:00-9:00 a.m.
    Dinner—1:15 p.m.
    Supper—5:30 p.m.
Meal Prices for Guests:
    Breakfast—$ .75
    Lunch—$ .85
    Dinner—$1.00
    Sunday dinner—$1.25

IV. Ann Carter Lee Hall

Terrace Room:
    Fountain Service:
    Monday through Friday:
    8:00 a.m.—9:45 p.m.
Saturday:
    8:00 a.m.—11:30 p.m.
Sunday:
    9:00 a.m.—9:00 p.m.

Meals:

Monday through Saturday:
    Breakfast—7:30-8:30 a.m.
    Lunch—12:30-1:30 p.m.
    Dinner—5:30-6:30 p.m.

Sunday:
    Breakfast—9:00-10:30 a.m.
    Dinner—12:30-2:00 p.m.

Book Store:

Monday through Saturday:
    8:00 a.m.—4:30 p.m.
    7:30 p.m.—8:45 p.m.

Sunday:
    3:00-4:30 p.m.
    7:30-8:45 p.m.

Pennant Rooms:
    Open at all hours.

Bowling Alleys:
    Every night (with the exception of Wednesday)
    7:00-10:15 p.m.
    Saturday, Sunday afternoons—2:00-5:30 p.m.

Note: Bowling is permitted only when an approved attendant is on duty. If there is no one in the bowling alley for over a period of 1 hour, the attendant may close the alley before the 5:30 or 10:15 hour.

Lounges: Open at all hours.

Ping Pong Room, Billiard Room, Shuffleboard Room:
Daily including Sunday:
1:00-5:30 p.m.
7:00-10:15 p.m. (with the exception of dance nights)
Swimming Pool:
Times will be posted by the Head of the Physical Education Department

V. College Infirmary
Doctor's Office Hours
Monday-Saturday: 1:30-2:30 p.m.
By appointment at times other than listed office hours.
By appointment only on Sunday
Student visiting hours—2-4 and 7-8 daily
Infirmary Office Hours:
Monday through Friday:
9:00 a.m.—4:00 p.m.
Saturday: 9:00 a.m.-12:00 noon
By appointment only on Sunday
Emergencies and bed patients may enter the infirmary at any time.

VI. College Post Office Pick-Ups
Daily and Saturday:
6:10 a.m.
8:30 a.m.
11:50 a.m.
4:45 p.m.
5:45 p.m.
Sundays and Holidays:
4:45 p.m.

AN EXPLANATION OF THE HONOR SYSTEM

The Honor System requires that a man or woman shall act honorably in all the relations and phases of student life. Lying, cheating, stealing, or breaking one's word of honor are considered infringements of the Honor System. The result in such cases will always be dishonorable dismissal from the college. The pledge in classes on quizzes, examinations, written problems, and exercises, means that the work which the student hands in to her professor is her own, which she herself has done in accordance with the requirements of the course as laid down by the professor. The pledge shall be as follows: **"I hereby declare upon my word of honor that I have neither given nor received help on this work."** The faculty will cooperate in establishing a clear understanding of these requirements. In any case of doubt as to the nature or extent of pledge the student should immediately request that the professor in charge make the requirements perfectly clear to the entire class.

The Honor System requires in the second place that, when a student sees another student in suspicious circumstances she shall investigate the matter as secretly and as speedily as possible and if she finds evidence of guilt, shall accuse the suspected student to her face. It is imperative that everyone recognize this duty of protecting the Honor System and the student body. Anyone who sees another student in suspicious circumstances and fails to investigate the matter is herself guilty of a breach of honor. Loyalty to the student body demands that one make this investigation. This can in no way be construed as spying or talebearing. It is the finest expression

13

of loyalty to a cherished tradition of honor among a community of self-governing students who wish to cooperate and work to the best interest of all concerned. The Honor Committee, duly elected by the students, represents the opinion of the students in this college and is in no way responsible to the faculty.

It is always advisable to associate two or three fellow students, if possible, in making an investigation. All materials having any connection with the case should be summarily taken possession of by the investigators, if need be against the wishes of the suspected person, as a matter of protection to all interests concerned. It is important to understand that the investigating students are the first to pass on the guilt or innocence of the suspected person; if they believe her to be guilty, they shall demand that the accused leave the college immediately; the right to appeal to the Honor Committee rests alone with the accused. In all fairness to a person accused, those who make the charges should have the precise breach of honor clearly fixed in their own minds. A student may not drop a charge upon the agreement of the accused to resign from the college; if a breach of honor is suspected, the ultimate result must be the quasi-public dishonorable dismissal in every case where the accused is believed to be guilty. Furthermore, if a student leaves the college "under a cloud" (for example, after being involved in cheating or some other dishonorable act) jurisdiction is retained by the students investigating the case. The student investigators shall give the suspected an opportunity to return and face the charge. If the accused refuses to return, the student investigators shall report to the chairman of the Honor Committee that such absent student is not entitled to an honorable dismissal.

It is also important that every student should exercise the greatest care to keep herself free from the suspicion of evil. Such practices as leaving the examination room for any length of time unaccompanied, or bringing text and note books into the examination room, or carelessly glancing toward another student's papers—these are heartily condemned by the Honor Committee. While such acts do not themselves constitute an infringement of the Honor System, such practices are highly dangerous both for the individual and for the continued well-being of the Honor System.

The Honor Committee earnestly discourages the use of pledges in all matters of personal concern; a woman's word of honor, once given, is inviolate, and its use in regulating trivialities is highly dangerous.

PROCEDURAL FEATURES

1. Any student believing that a breach of the Honor System has been committed shall, with the assistance of such students of the college as she may desire to call upon, investigate the matter as secretly and speedily as possible. After a thorough investigation, if they believe the suspected person guilty of a violation of honor, they shall demand that she explain her conduct. In case the investigating group is satisfied that the suspected student is not guilty of improper conduct, there shall be no further proceedings, and nothing connected with the case shall be made public. If, after hearing her explanation, or after she has refused to make an explanation, the investigators are still con-

15

vinced of her guilt, they shall demand that she leave the college at once.

2. The accused must then either leave the college or demand of the chairman of the Honor Committee that the Honor Committee be convened to try the case. The case shall be tried as soon thereafter as is conveniently possible, giving primary consideration to the wishes of the accused.

3. In case the accused leaves the college without trial by the Honor Committee, the accuser shall notify the chairman of the Honor Committee of the name of the offender and the nature of the offense. Following such a notification, the Honor Committee shall take action to record the facts in the same manner as if the case had been tried before them. The status of the accused under such circumstances is the same as though she had been found guilty by the Honor Committee.

4. The Honor Committee shall consist primarily of the presidents of the four classes and a president who shall be elected by the student body. When sitting upon a trial, the house president of the dormitory in which the accused resides, or in case of an off-campus student, the off-campus representative, shall constitute the sixth member of the committee. Until the Freshman Class president is elected, the vice-president of the Senior Class shall serve in her place. In case of absence of any member of this committee, the next highest ranking officer in the class shall act in her place, the officers ranking in the following order —president, vice-president, secretary, treasurer, and historian.

5. On the trial of a case, the president of the

16

Honor Council shall act as chairman. The minutes of the trial shall be kept by an employed stenographer. These minutes shall be in the custody of the Honor Committee, and it shall be their duty to see that they are properly stored for safe keeping from year to year.

The minutes of the trial shall be open to inspection by any person who may satisfy the Honor Committee of his legitimate interest in the case. No notes or memoranda shall be permitted to be made from the minutes. During any inspection of those minutes, there shall always be present at least two members of the Honor Committee.

6. On conviction of the accused, the chairman shall report the name of the convicted student and the nature of the offense of which she was found guilty to the Registrar, who shall notify her professors, parents, and the Dean of Women. In case the accused is declared innocent, the minutes of the trial shall be immediately destroyed. It shall be within the discretion of the Honor Committee to give such publicity of the facts of a case resulting in a finding of guilt as shall be considered advisable.

7. At the trial before the Honor Committee, both sides may be represented by counsel from the student body, but not otherwise.

8. If, after thorough trial, four of the five persons who compose the Honor Committee are convinced of the guilt of the accused and shall so cast their vote in a secret ballot, the accused must leave the college immediately.

9. From the decision of the Honor Committee there shall be no appeal.

10. A case resulting in a verdict of guilty may be reopened only upon the production of new evidence bearing directly on the question of guilt. Any person seeking to reopen a case shall appear before the Honor Committee and state the nature of the evidence. The committee shall then consider whether the evidence is sufficiently relevant to warrant a retrial. If a case is reopened, it shall be entirely retried. For the purposes of this section, the composition of the Honor Committee in cases of petition for retrial shall be governed by the provisions of Section 4 of the Procedural Features of this code and no other. No member of the committee entitled to sit under the provisions of Section 4 above shall be precluded from exercisisng such rights by virtue of his absence from the first trial.

11. A definite time shall be set aside to explain the principles of the Honor System to new students. The speaker for this occasion shall be selected by the Honor Committee. A copy of the Honor System shall be in the **Bayonet** and the first edition of the college paper. A brief outline of the procedure of the Honor System shall be given to each student.

REGISTRATION AS A STUDENT IN THE COLLEGE IS NOT CONSIDERED TO HAVE BEEN COMPLETED UNTIL THE PLEDGE CARD HAS BEEN SIGNED. NO GRADES OR CREDITS WILL BE RELEASED UNLESS THE SIGNED HONOR PLEDGE CARD IS ON FILE.

Honor Committee President—Patsy Preston

HONOR CODE

I, as a student and citizen of Mary Washington College, do hereby resolve to uphold the honor of the college by refraining from giving or receiving academic material in a manner not authorized by the instructor; from the illegal appropriation of the property of others; and from the deliberate falsification of facts. I shall do all in my power at all times to create a spirit of honesty and honor for its own sake both by upholding the Honor System myself and by helping others to do so.

(Signed)..

ADMINISTRATIVE POLICIES

The Student Council under the advice, guidance, and supervision of Joint Council, serves as a link between the administration and the student body. The Student Government, subject to approval of the administrative authorities, assumes responsibility for carrying out the provisions of the Handbook and for promoting personal responsibility, loyalty, and a high sense of honor in individual students.

The administration of the college is held responsible by the State and by the public for the discipline and welfare of the students, and is vested with the authority and responsibility of enforcing regulations in the event of default on the part of Student Council or Joint Council.

The college reserves the right to request any student whose conduct or general attitude is considered unsatisfactory and not in keeping with the standards and traditions of the college to withdraw, even though no specific charge is made against her.

Hostesses.—Hostesses in the various dormitories and residence halls represent the college authorities and are responsible for the orderly administration of the respective dormitories or residence over which they preside.

Student officials or the House Council are expected to cooperate with the hostesses in carrying out the dormitory regulations.

Student Clubs and Organizations.—Administrative approval must be secured for the establishment of any club or new student organization on the campus.

Faculty Sponsors.—All faculty sponsors of classes or student organizations must be approved by the administration.

Programs and Performances.—All public programs or performances given at the college or anywhere else, either by the faculty or students, must be approved by the Committee on Theatrical Standards.

Appropriation or Subsidy.—The college administration reserves the right to withdraw any appropriation or subsidy to any student organization or publication which does not conform to the traditions and standards of the college, that tends to portray the college in an unfair and unfavorable light, and that is not in keeping with academic dignity.

STUDENT COUNCIL 1956-57

Officers

President	Emmy Hepford
Vice-President	Meg Patton
Secretary	Evelyn Nitti
Treasurer	Sandy Elroy

Representatives

Senior	Jackie McClung
Junior	Ebbie Breedon
Sophomore	Mary Jones
Freshman	To Be Elected
Town Girl	Betsy Powers

House Presidents

Ball	Lois Prime
Custis	Betty Mae Rose
Madison	Barbara Stroop
Westmoreland	Marcia Boyles
Mason	Helen Theophilos
Randolph	Jane Crenshaw
Virginia	Fran Karins
Betty Lewis	Isabel Gill
Willard	Peggy Kelley
Cornell	Carol Buskell

Ex Officio

Y. W. C. A.	Audrey Neff
R. A.	Barbara Zimmer

Freshman Counselors

Betty Lewis	Lucille Geoghegan
Cornell	Elsie Minix
Willard	Bev Cook
	Mary Jane Prillaman
	Marie Clauditis

22

STUDENT GOVERNMENT ASSOCIATION ORGANIZATION

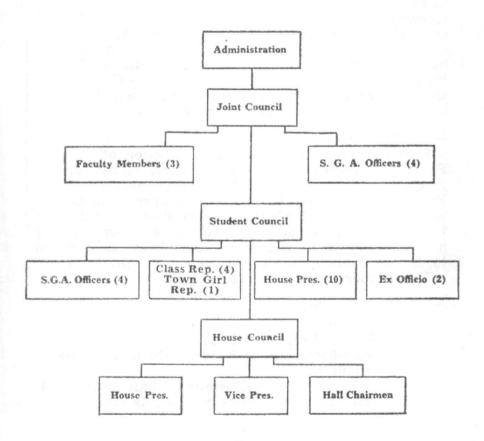

RULES AND REGULATIONS OF THE STUDENT GOVERNMENT ASSOCIATION

Mary Washington College wants only citizens who are willing to cooperate with its democratic program. If any student fails to abide by the legislation of our student body, the offense will be seriously regarded and subject to penalties ranging from a denial of social privileges to expulsion at the discretion of the Student Council and Joint Council. A Mary Washington girl is considered a lady and is expected to uphold the standards of her college. The following rules and regulations formulated in accordance with Article IX of the Constitution shall be effective on and after September, 1956. All regulations are subject to class privileges.

I. Dormitory:

Each dormitory is under the jurisdiction of a House President, supported by representatives elected or appointed from each Hall. This group, plus the Vice-President of Student Government, comprises the dormitory House Council which is responsible for enforcing the social regulations of the college and for creating a community spirit within the dormitory. In addition to House Council, in the Freshman dormitories there will be upperclassmen to act as counselors.

A. House Council:

1. Personnel:
   a. House President—Chairman.
   b. Vice-President of Student Council—Advisory member.
   c. Hall Chairmen—Dormitory hall representatives who shall elect within this group a dor-

24

mitory vice president, secretary, treasurer and and social chairman.

2. Duties:
   a. Must handle designated disciplinary problems that arise concerning a member of their dormitory.
   b. May refer cases to the Student Council if the House Council deems it necessary.
   c. A student may have the right of appeal to the Student Council.
   d. Cooperate with hostess in maintaining order.

3. Specified duties:
   a. House President—acts as chairman; has no vote.
   b. Dormitory Vice-President — assists House President and serves in her absence.
   c. Dormitory Secretary—takes minutes of meetings and cases.
      All cases must be posted on the dormitory bulletin board for a period of one week; a copy of each offense and punishment must be given the dormitory hostess and the Vice-President of Student Council.
   d. Dormitory Treasurer—collects dormitory dues and handles all monetary matters of the dormitory.
   e. Social Chairman—shall work in coordination with the House President and Hostess in planning dormitory social activities.

4. Meetings:
   a. House Council—shall meet every Thursday at 10:30 p.m.

b. Each member of House Council must be present at the meeting.
5. Election:
   a. Hall Chairmen—shall be elected each semester (time designated by the House President) in the following manner:
   The House President shall present a slate of two nominees from each hall. Further nominations shall be made from the floor. The hall chairmen will be elected by members of the respective halls.
   b. Vice-President, Secretary, Treasurer, and Social Chairman will be elected from hall chairmen.
6. Phones will not be used after 11:00 p.m. except in emergencies.
7. Students living in dormitories where there are no pay phones must reverse the charges on long distance calls.
8. In case of emergency, permission may be received in advance to make long distance calls on the hostess' phone in the dormitories where there are no pay phones.
9. No student may leave her dormitory before 5:00 a.m.
10. If a student has a date calling before 9:00 a.m., she is responsible for meeting him. There will be no entertaining in the parlor before 9:00 a.m.

B. Dormitory Hours:
1. Each student is required to keep the following study hours: Monday through Friday— 7:30 p.m. to 10:15 p.m.

2. Each student is required to keep the following quiet hours: Monday through Friday—11:00 p.m. to 8:30 a.m.
Saturday midnight until 9:00 a.m. on Sunday.
3. Radios and phonographs may be played during quiet hours but only if low enough not to be heard in adjoining rooms.
4. Students are not to take baths after 12:00 midnight.
5. Students must be in their dormitories by 11:00 p.m. Sundays through Fridays, and Saturdays by 12:00 midnight.
6. Seniors will be allowed two Saturday one o'clocks per semester.
7. When returning to campus after the official college holidays, students must be in their dormitories by 12:00 midnight.
8. No student is at any time permitted to admit anyone or to leave a dormitory after closing hours except with permission.

C. Rooms:

1. Rooms must be in order at all times, including the disposal of rubbish and empty containers.
2. Permission must be received from the Director of Dormitories:
   (a) to remove furniture from rooms.
   (b) to take down a bed.
3. All articles desired on the walls must be hung from the molding. No nails, tacks, glue, or tape may be used on the walls. Clothes hangers must not be hung on the light fixtures.
4. Cooking and ironing are not allowed in the in-

dividual rooms; special rooms are provided for this purpose.

5. Valuables and money may be kept in the Bursar's office. The college is not responsible for them otherwise.

6. Men visitors are never allowed in any student's room wtihout permission from the dormitory hostess.

7. Trunks are not permitted in rooms. They must be packed and unpacked in the storage rooms.

8. Any food kept must be stored in a glass or metal container.

9. No food or beverages may be sold in dormitories except prepackaged candy bars, cookies, and the like, which may be sold at designated places by organizations with the permission of the Dean of Women.

10. Any sales solicitation by individuals or organizaations must be approved by the Dean of Women.

11. On Saturdays a student may spend the night in dormitories other than her own by checking with her own hostess when leaving, and with the hostess of the other dormitory upon her arrival.

12. When exchanging rooms within the dormitory on Saturday night, a student must sign in and out with her hostess and on sign-out card.

13. When a student wishes to entertain guests overnight in the dormitory during the week, special permission must be secured from the Dean of Women. No overnight guests will be permitted during examination periods.

14. No pets are allowed in dormitories.

D. Laundry:

1. Laundry will be collected and re-delivered to all the dormitories.
2. Laundry bags are absolutely prohibited in any of the buildings and on the grounds of the college except in the dormitories and laundry building.
3. Claims for lost laundry must be reported to the laundry within three days after receipt, and laundry slips must be presented.
4. When receiving laundry other than your own, return it to your head resident.

E. Lights:

1. Freshmen and Sophomores must have their lights out at 12:00 midnight, except on Saturdays. No light cuts shall be granted.
2. Juniors must have their lights out by 1 o'clock, except on Saturdays. No light cuts shall be granted.
3. Saturday night there will be no light restrictions except for Freshmen who may have lights on until 1:00 a.m. All students must observe quiet hour after 12:00 midnight on Saturday.
4. Seniors have no light restrictions, except during final semester exams.
5. All students are expected to get an adequate amount of sleep and if the privilege of lights is abused, strict legislation will be immediately enacted.
6. Lights must be out promptly at 1:00 a.m. during final semester exams. This applies to all classes.
7. On the final night of class benefits, with the ex-

ception of Saturday, lights in the respective dormitories of the class involved must be out at 1:00 a.m. This does not apply to Seniors.
8. Lights may be turned on at 5:00 a.m.

F. Signing Out:

Each student must sign herself out and in at all times. The student must return by the closing hour of the day and date recorded on the Sign Out Card. She must sign in immediately upon her return. Signing after closing hours counts as late minutes.
1. Sign out cards are to be used:
  a. When leaving Fredericksburg:
    (1) for the weekend (must leave before 7:00 p.m.)
    (2) for overnight (must leave before 7:00 p.m.)
        (a) at home during week, get special permission from hostess and have her initial card.
        (b) other than home, get special permission from the Dean of Women.
    (3) for the day during the week (must leave before 4:30 p.m.)
        (a) at home, get special permission from hostess and have her initial card.
        (b) other than home, get special permission from Dean of Women.
    (4) for Saturday and Sunday (leaving before 4:30 p.m.)
  b. When dating (riding and campus included)
  c. When not returning to campus until after 6:00 p.m.

30

d. When spending night out of dormitory.
    (1) in another dormitory on Saturday night
    (2) during school vacations
    (3) in the infirmary
e. When going to Quantico on Friday, Saturday, or Sunday.
f. When visiting in Fredericksburg:
    (1) to spend night in town with immediate family, get special permission from hostess and have her initial card.
    (2) to visit in a private home in town or in a ten mile radius for the day or evening. If this involves a date, get permission from hostess and have her initial card.

2. Reservations must be made in the Dean of Women's Office by 5:00 p.m. Thursday when spending the weekend in Charlottesville.

G. Special Permission Must Be Obtained:

1. From Hostess:
    a. to admit anyone, leave or come in a dormitory after closing hours.
    b. to allow male members of family to visit room.
    c. to go home for the day or overnight during the week.
    d. to spend night in town with immediate family
    e. to visit in a private home in town or a ten-mile vicinity for the day until 10:30 p.m. with a date
    f. to change destination after signing out
    g. to return at time other than sign out card indicates.

31

2. From Dean of Women:
   a. to sell prepackaged candy bars, cookies, and the like at designated places by organizations
   b. to leave Fredericksburg for the day or overnight during the week for places other than home.
   c. for special use of cars (only seniors, and for other extreme cases.)
3. From President of Student Government:
   a. to change destination after signing out.
   b. to return at time other than sign out card indicates.
   c. to wear bermudas, etc. to college sponsored picnics and sports.
4. From Parents:
   Written permission stating the name of the hotel, motel, etc. must be presented to the hostess for each visit to hotel, etc. in cities other than Washington and Charlottesville.
5. From Director of the Dormitories:
   Permission to remove furniture from rooms.
   Permission to take down beds.

H. Parlors:
   1. Dormitory parlors may be used for the following purposes:
      a. Entertaining guests.
      b. Class and house meetings.
      c. Vespers.
   2. Dormitory parlors may not be used for the following purposes:
      a. Club meetings, recitals, and entertainments.
      b. Eating and dancing at any time.
      c. Card playing on Sundays.

I. Fire Drills:

1. The Fire Commander elected by the student body shall supervise the fire drills held at regular intervals throughout the year.
2. At the time of the fire drill, students are responsible for the following:
   a. Wearing laced shoes and full length coats.
   b. Taking two towels.
   c. Closing all windows.
   d. Completely raising window shades.
   e. Closing transoms.
   f. Leaving on lights.
   g. Closing the door.
   h. Walking quietly to place designated by the Fire Commander.
3. Any student failing to leave for a fire drill is subject to punishment by House Council.
4. Only the Fire Commander and her assistants shall sound the alarm, except in case of fire.

J. Taxis:

1. Taxis may call for and unload passengers at any dormitory except Virginia Hall. Residents of this dormitory are to meet their cabs in Chandler Circle.
2. Students hiring a taxi to take them out of town must register with their hostess.

K. Signing Up For Rooms:

1. Registration fees must be paid by the date designated by the College.
2. Only those having paid by the above date will be allowed to draw for rooms first. Those who

are late paying will draw after the above have signed for their rooms.

3. Numbers may not be traded.
4. Students must live in dormitories designated according to classes.
5. The maximum room occupancy recommended by the Dean of Women's Office will be observed.
6. Suites must not be signed for unless you have selected suitemates.
7. Students may not sign up anyone as a roommate or suitemate who has not paid her registration fee by the designated date.
8. Any vacancy left in a room may be filled at the discretion of the Dean of Women.

II. Campus Life:

A. Activities Available to Students:

1. Ann Carter Lee Hall:
   a. Indoor swimming pool at designated hours.
   b. Billiard Room.
   c. Ping Pong Room.
   d. Bowling Alley.
   e. Recreation Rooms for indoor games.
   f. Pennant Rooms.
   g. Lounges.
   h. Gothic Room.
2. Movies in George Washington Hall.
3. Benefits in Monroe Hall.
4. Plays in duPont Hall.
5. Monday through Saturday students may engage in the following sports facilities at all times. On Sunday they may be used after 1:00 p.m.

a. Outdoor swimming pools at designated times. Framar and Trench Hill pools for residents of those dormitories only.
b. Golf.
c. Tennis.
d. Horse-back Riding.
6. Picnics: Students in groups of four, or when double dating, may go on picnics until 6:00 p.m.
7. Regulations concerning sun-bathing are as follows:
   a. Sun-bathing is permitted only (1) in the immediate area of the outdoor swimming pool when swimming; (2) in the designated areas behind duPont and Framar; (3) at Trench Hill and Tri-Unit ramps for residents only.
   b. Sun-bathing is not permitted on Sunday except for residents of Tri-Unit.
   c. Sun-bathers must be properly clad while sun-bathing and must wear a skirt or dress when going to and from the sun-bathing areas.
8. Regulations concerning serenading are as follows:
   a. A serenade chairman will be elected by each dormitory and will be in charge of the following:
      (1) Planning the serenade.
      (2) Securing permission from the Dean of Women by 5:00 p.m. of the selected day.
      (3) Notifying the hostesses of the dormitories involved.
      (4) Conducting the serenade.
   b. The hours for the serenades shall be between 10:15 and 10:45 p.m.

35

c. The serenaders may enter only the parlors of the dormitories or remain outside, as they prefer.

d. Orderly conduct shall be observed at all times.

e. Serenaders and those being serenaded must be properly dressed.

9. College Dances:

a. Dances shall end by 11:59 p.m. on Saturday in compliance with Virginia law.

b. After this hour the Dean of Women may give permission for refreshments to be served.

c. Should breakfast follow the formal dance, students must be in their dormitories by 2:00 a.m.

d. Students who do not attend breakfast or who leave the breakfast before 1:30 must return immediately to their own dormitories.

e. Students may stroll in lighted areas during formal and informal dances until 11:59 p.m.

f. Dance dates may remain in parlors after dances until the closing hour.

g. Formal attire is required for both students and dates at formal dances.

h. Following a dance, students from Betty Lewis have ten additional minutes to get back to the dormitory; students from Cornell and Trench Hill have fifteen additional minutes.

10. Students may leave the campus after dances and class benefits only with their immediate families or guardians. Exceptions may be granted by the Dean of Women at the written request of the parents.

B. Smoking:

Smokers are held strictly responsible for any damage to college property and smoking in unauthorized places by anyone is a very serious offense.

1. Smoking is permitted in:
   a. Dormitory rooms.
   b. Day students' room in Chandler Hall.
   c. Pennant Rooms and Terrace Room.
   d. Room 8 in duPont Hall.
   e. Off-campus dining places with dinner or a snack.
   f. Lounges in Ann Carter Lee Hall for guests only.
   g. Parlors and Recreation Rooms of dormitories for guests only.
2. Students are prohibited from smoking in all other places including the college bus and taxis.

C. Drinking:

Drinking of intoxicating beverages is not condoned at any time.

The possession or drinking of intoxicating beverages within a thirty mile radius is considered a most serious offense.

1. Drinking is prohibited:
   a. On campus and within a thirty mile radius.
   b. At all beaches, parks, and resorts.
   c. At Quantico except on Saturday night or when remaining overnight.

2. **At no time may a student return to the college with alcohol on her breath or under the influence of alcohol. This is a serious offense and subject to discipline by Student Council.**

D. Dining Halls:

1. Attendance:

   Students are required to be on time at all meals in order to cooperate with student waitresses.

2. Student Hostesses:

   a. A Senior or Junior will preside over each table and may invite students to sit with her.
   b. The student hostess will dismiss her table at lunch; each dining room is dismissed as a whole at dinner by the hostess in charge.
   c. Etiquette and good conduct shall be maintained by the student hostess at her table.

3. Announcements:

   a. Only announcements which concern a large portion of the student body may be made in the dining halls.
   b. There must be complete quiet when announcements are made.

4. Clothing:

   a. No head scarves or curlers are to appear in the dining halls except at breakfast, when scarves must cover pin curls.
   b. Socks should not be worn for the noonday meals on Sunday.
   c. Students wearing riding habits will eat in a designated dining hall.
   d. All coats must be hung in the coat rooms if not worn. They are not to be left on the backs of chairs, the floor, in the Dome Room, etc.

III. Off Campus Regulations:

A student is under the jurisdiction of the college at all times, and is held directly responsible to the college for her deportment while away on weekend visits or enroute to and from the college. Students visiting away from the college or in the homes of their friends will not be expected to adhere to all detailed handbook regulations, such as dinner dates, going to movies, riding in automobiles, etc.

All parents will receive a form which they will be asked to fill out and return to the Dean of Women. This gives them the opportunity to grant their daughter either general permission covering all absences from campus or limited permission in which they may specify their own restrictions. This includes dating and riding privileges and is subject to change according to parents' wishes. The college reserves the right of final authority in all cases involving absences from the campus.

A. General Regulations:

1. Reading Day:
    a. To leave town: Students must obtain permission from the Dean of Women.
    b. To leave the campus: Students may go to town; must return to campus before 6:00 p.m.
2. No student may leave for overnight after 7:00 p.m. except by special permission from her hostess or the President of Student Government. All such permissions shall be duly recorded. This does not apply to leaving before a holiday.

3. When a change of destination occurs, or when unable to return to the campus at the expected time, a student herself must request permission from one of the following:
   a. Hostess of her dormitory.
   b. President of Student Government.
4. When not going directly to designated destination from college, a student must indicate stops to be made before destination is reached.
5. Each student must sign herself out and in at all times.
6. Snacks:
   a. Girls in groups of four may visit Howard Johnson's, the Hot Shoppe, Alman's and Scotty's for a snack, allowing themselves ample time to return to campus by dormitory closing hours.
   b. Monday through Thursday this counts as a night in town

B. **Trips to Town:**
1. Any student may go to town during the day without signing out provided she returns to the campus by 6:00 p.m.
2. Students leaving the campus after this hour hour must be properly signed out according to class privileges:
   a. Freshman and Sophomores: Two nights a month in groups of four.
   b. Juniors and Seniors: Four nights a month in groups of three.
3. Students may go to church on Sunday night according to the above class groupings unless going

by car or taxi. This does not count as a night in town.

4. Appropriate dress is expected in town as well as on the campus.

5. Students may attend the movies or other approved entertainment in town at any time except Saturday and Sunday nights in according with class privileges.

6. Students may have their evening meal in town any night returning by 6:00 p.m. unless otherwise signed out.

7. Students should for safety reasons cross the highway at Snowden Street when going to Howard Johnson's.

C. Visiting in a Private Home:

1. Students may have dinner in a home in town or may spend the day, informing hostess that the invitation has been extended. If this involves a date, special permission must be granted by the hostess.

2. These students must sign in and out in their dormitories and return by dormitory closing hour.

3. Students must return immediately to the college after leaving the home of their hostess.

4. Students may visit in private homes during the day, provided they sign out on the sign out card.

5. A student may be granted permission by the hostess to spend the weekend in town with her parents.

D. Out of Town Trips:
1. When an absence from the campus will include days on which the student has scheduled classes, the absence must be approved in the following manner:
   a. Hostess if class cuts are available.
   b. Doctor if leaving for medical reasons.
   c. Dean of College if academic excuse is not covered by a medical excuse.
   d. Dean of Women for other reasons for leaving.
   e. In absence of any of the above, the Dean of College or Dean of Women, shall have power to act.
2. When girls are signing out for home during the week, the hostess may grant the permission.
3. Students may take unlimited weekends provided there is no conflict with class schedule or college obligations.
4. Seniors may leave for the day Monday through Friday without permission if they return by 6:00 p.m.
5. Students may visit neighboring cities on Saturday and Sunday, signing out no later than 4:30 p.m. and returning by dormitory closing hours.
6. In neighboring cities students may spend the night in the following places only:
   a. Homes of friends or relatives.
   b. In Washington:
      (1) Meridian Hotel
   c. In Richmond:
      (1) Tourist homes approved by the Dean of Women
   d. In Charlottesville: Places approved by the social committees of the University of Virginia.

42

e. In Quantico:
   (1) Waller Hall
   (2) The Hostess' House
f. In Dahlgren: Tourist homes approved by the Dean of Women.
g. When visiting in other cities, students may stay in hotels, motels, etc. only with special written permission (naming the hotel, etc.) from home, presented to the hostess for each visit.

7. Students must comply with the following regulations when staying anywhere in Charlottesville:
   a. Room arrangements must be made in the Dean of Women's Office not later than 5:00 p.m. on Thursday, and they may not be changed by students or dates except with permission of the Dean of Women at Mary Washington or the University of Virginia.
   b. Students must be in one hour after the feature dance; otherwise by 2:00 a.m.
   c. On Sunday nights they must be in by 12:00 midnight.
   d. Upon arrival at Charlottesville, a student must notify her hostess in person or by telephone promptly.
   e. Students must remain in their approved homes until at least 7:00 a.m.
   f. Students must comply with rules set up by the Social Committee of the University at any time and under any circumstances when visiting there.

8. Students may spend Saturday or Sunday at a neighboring beach except Colonial Beach, which may be visited by girls with dates only.

9. Students must leave the beach by 6:00 p.m.
10. Students returning from trips must come directly to the college after entering the city limits of Fredericksburg, unless stopping to eat or accompanied by relatives.

E. **Walks:**

1. Students may go for walks outside the city limits in groups of four or more on any day.
2. Students with dates or in groups of two may stroll or visit historic places in town.
3. Anyone taking these walks must return by 6:00 p.m.

F. **Marine Ball:**

Due to insufficient housing at Quantico, students attending the annual Marine Ball are not permitted to spend the night. Dates may call for the girls but the girls will return to the College following the Ball on the College bus.

IV. **Dating:**

A. **General Regulations:**

1. All students without general permission from their parents must have a calling list of approved escorts.
2. Men who disregard the standards and regulations of the college will be removed from the calling list by the Dean of Women. It is the policy of this college to discourage drinking at all times. Any caller on whose breath the odor of alcohol is apparent or whose conduct gives evidence of drinking will be warned and asked to leave im-

44

mediately. Any repetition will result in the removal of calling privileges. Students are expected to acquaint callers with the above regulations.

3. The Guest Card:
   a. Dates must secure guest cards from the dormitory hostess where the student lives.
   b. On the first visit dates remaining in Fredericksburg and the ten mile radius will be given a temporary guest card which must be . returned to the hostess at the end of the evening.
   c. After the first visit a permanent guest card card may be obtained which must be shown to the hostess each visit.

4. Students must sign out at any time, when dating on campus or leaving campus with a date. This does not pertain to dating in the parlor.

5. Local Men:
   a. "Local" men shall be interpreted as those living within a thirty mile radius of the college including Quantico, A. P. Hill, Dahlgren, etc.
   b. Local dating includes Fredericksburg and the ten mile vicinity.
   c. Seniors only may date local men on any night.
   d. Underclassmen may date local men on Friday, Saturday, and Sunday only.
   e. Local men may date students for Lyceums and other special programs (as determined by the Dean of Women).
   g. Anyone disregarding the above will be removed from the calling list.

6. Students must not be in the company of unapproved escorts.

7. Riding in cars:
   a. Within a ten-mile radius of Fredericksburg is permitted under the following conditions:
      (1) Freshmen and Sophomores: One couple may ride to and from designated destination.
      (2) Juniors or Seniors may ride without a destination with dates any afternoon until 6:00 p.m. After 6:00 p.m. riding must be to and from a designated destination only.
      (3) For all rides with dates, students must sign in and out.
      (4) A student living in an off-campus dormitory may ride with her date to the campus for any college sponsored function or meal.
   b. Girls must not sit in cars on campus with men callers at any time.
   c. Students who attend movies in town at night with dates may have a snack before returning to campus.
   d. Any violation of riding privileges is considered one of the most serious offense and is punishable accordingly.

B. On Campus:
   1. Strolling during the day is permitted anywhere on the campus.
   At night strolling is not permitted in the following places:
   a. Area surrounding the dining hall including the bridge and path to duPont.
   b. Area surrounding the library including the amphitheater.

46

    c. Area surrounding the infirmary including the tennis courts, hockey field, and cabin.

    d. Area surrounding Framar.

2. All recreational facilities, excluding the swimming pools, are available except during class hours. Fees for horseback riding will be paid directly to the stables.

3. Dances, entertainments, and movies sponsored by the College are offered.

4. The facilities in Ann Carter Lee Hall are available for students and dates.

5. A student may entertain in the dormitory parlor of the building in which she lives, excluding Custis and Madison.

C. Off Campus:

1. Movies may be attended at any time except Saturday night and Sunday night.

2. Students with escorts may have snacks in town returning by dormitory closing hours.

3. Historic shrines may be visited.

4. Friday, Saturdays, and Sundays students may go to Quantico for the evening, leaving no later than 8:00 p.m. from the College.

5. Beaches may be visited with a date until 6:00 p.m. on Saturday and Sunday.

6. Neighboring cities may be visited with dates for the day on Saturdays and Sundays, signing out no later than 4:30 p.m. and returning by dormitory closing hour.

7. Picnics: When double-dating, students may go on picnics until 6:00 p.m.

V. Out of Bounds:

A. The following off-campus places are out of bounds:
1. The Pony
2. Drive-in Theater
3. Colonial Beach for girls without dates.

B. Students may not stroll at night in the areas stated "Dating, IV., B., 1."

VI. Miscellaneous:

A. Protection and Preservation of College Property:

1. Students are held strictly responsible for damage to buildings and equipment through carelessness or otherwise.

2. The cutting of flowers or shrubs for room decoration or for any other purpose, or the mutilation of trees by cutting, breaking, or attaching posters is strictly prohibited, and anyone committing such an offense will be required to make proper restitution.

3. The use of candles or any other type of lighting which constitutes a fire hazard is prohibited. No candles are to be used in any of the buildings or on the campus except in the dining halls and the Terrace Room under close supervision.

4. Any floral or decorative seasonal arrangements are not to be removed by any unauthorized person.

5. The College is not responsible for the personal property of the students, no matter what the cause or nature of the damage. Families may carry such insurance as they deem necessary.

B. Telephones:
1. Public telephones are located in Chandler, Ann Carter Lee Hall, duPont Hall, Monroe Hall, and George Washington Hall.
2. Dormitory telephone regulations may be found under "Dormitory Hours."

C. Lounging:
Students may not lounge in an unlady-like manner on the campus grounds.

D. Dress:
1. Students are expected to observe neatness, appropriateness, and good taste in personal appearances on all occasions, both formal and informal.
2. Students are expected to "dress" for Sunday noon meal.
3. Formal dress is expected for Lyceums and specified dinners, unless semi-formal dress is announced.
4. Unconventional apparel is prohibited in the class rooms, studios, laboratories, in the dining room on the campus.
5. Students may use their own discretion in wearing apparel within the dormitory (subject to House rules).
6. Special permission will be given by the Student Government President for the wearing of slacks, Bermuda shorts, and pedal pushers only to college sponsored picnics, sleigh rides, scene shop, on the golf course, tennis courts, and to the Cabin. This attire must be covered by a skirt, except at the approved destination.

49

7. Riding Habit:
   a. May be worn only during riding classes and when going to and from the stables, except when there is not time to change before other classes and meals.
   b. May not appear in the Student Activities Building after 7:00 unless they have been to a Convo or required meeting. Exception: May patronize the Book Store any night after 7:00 if they have absolutely not had time to change their riding habit.
   c. Is not to be worn in the Terrace Room after 7:00 p.m. on Friday and Saturday, and not at all on Sunday.
   d. Must not be worn in the parlor at all unless for class meeting or when passing through.
   e. Must not be worn down town unless for authorized activities.
   f. Must not be worn in the dining hall on Sunday for the noon meal unless a formal hunt is planned.
   g. Is limited to students taking equitation.
   h. Must include shoes when jodphurs are worn, but boots when breeches are worn.

E. **Illness:**
   1. If a student is too ill to attend meals or classes, she should report to the college infirmary where she can obtain medical attention.
   2. In order to be excused from classes when going home for medical attention, the excuse must be submitted to the infirmary before leaving.
   3. If a student is ill after the dormitory closing

50

hours, she must notify her hostess, who will notify the infirmary to admit her immediately.

4. A student must not leave the infirmary without the permission of the nurse or doctor.
5. A student may call a local doctor of her choice after notifying the infirmary. The fee is then paid by the student.

F. Graduation:
1. Students must remain in their own dormitories.
2. All students remaining for graduation are under college jurisdiction.

G. Post Office:
Students are asked to enter the right door and to leave by the left door.

H. Marriages.
Students who marry during the school year are required to notify the Dean of Women immediately. Failure to do so is a serious offense.

VII. Automobiles:
Riding with anyone to whom the college has refused its social courtesies, or with anyone whom the college considers undesirable is forbidden. No student may accept pick-up rides except those specified below. Any violation of this privilege is considered one of the most serious offenses and is punishable accordingly.

A. Possession and Use:
1. Only Seniors may bring an automobile to college; such cars must be registered in the office of the Dean of Women.

51

2. Seniors may use their cars to go away for the day during the week with permission from the hostess. They may also leave for the day on Saturdays, and Sundays, and for the weekend without permission.
3. Seniors may use their own cars locally until 6:00 p.m. After 6:00 they must sign out for designated destination.
4. Written permission must be granted from parents for a Senior to have a car on campus or to operate a car locally.

B. **General Regulations concerning riding:**
   1. Students may ride with the following:
      a. Dates, in accordance with general dating rules.
      b. Members of the immediate family.
      c. Town students.
      d. Administration, Faculty or their wives and/or husbands.
      e. Seniors.
      f. Townspeople to and from church.
      g. Parents of other students.
   2. Students may travel in a hired conveyance, registering with their hostess if the ride will take them out of the bounds permitted by the college. For example: Hiring taxis to go out of town.
   3. Riding under other circumstances must be with permission from the Dean of Women.

VIII. Convocation and Assembly:
   All students shall be seated alphabetically and according to classes by the Student Government Association. Every student is expected to be in attendance at these exercises and in her assigned seat

52

unless taking cuts, or unless excusd because of ill-
nes or for other valid reasons.

A. Assembly:
1. Held on Mondays at 12:30 p.m.
2. Each student is entitled to 3 cuts a semester.

B. Convocation:
1. Held on Wednesdays at 7:00 p.m.
2. Each student is entitled to 2 cuts a semester.
3. One convocation a month is compulsory for student body meetings.

C. Student Body Meetings:
1. Special student body meetings, as announced
may be held on Thursday at 12:30 p.m.
2. Attendance will be required; an absence is counted as 2 cuts.

D. Absences:
1. Cuts cannot be carried over from one semester
to another.
2. Student Government is entirely responsible for
reporting absences.
3. After one overcut, a set of class cuts shall be
forfeited.
4. After two overcuts, the student shall be called
before Student Council.
5. Attendance at certain programs may be required.
Those not attending will be charged with double
cuts.
6. All formal Convocations are compulsory for
Seniors.
7. The Dean may excuse students from Convocation
and Assembly for essential business.

53

8. The President of Student Government may excuse students from student body meetings for essential business.

E. Orientation for New Students:
Students are entitled to one cut in the Orientation programs.

IX. Class Organization:
A. Dues:
1. Must be paid by November 15 for upperclassmen and by December 15 for Freshmen.
2. Neglect of paying dues will result in the deprivation of the following privileges:
   a. Voting
   b. Holding any office
   c. Participating in class functions
   d. Having pictures in the annual
   e. Receiving cap and gown.

B. Sponsor:
1. Class sponsors shall be elected by the class.
2. The upperclasses may meet and organize prior to the appointment of the class sponsor.
3. The class program for the year shall not be undertaken until the class sponsor has been elected.

C. Benefits:
1. The Vice-President of each class shall be the director of the benefit given annually by the class.
2. The months for the benefits shall be as follows:
   a. Seniors—November
   b. Juniors—February

c. Sophomores—March

d. Freshmen—April

3. A student-faculty committee will review each benefit. After class benefits have been approved by this committee, they shall be given only as approved. This committee shall consist of the Dean of Women, the Vice-President of Student Government, and the four SGA Class Representatives.

4. Room 1 duPont Hall is provided for painting scenery for benefits.

X. Violations of Regulations:

All decisions of the House Council shall be posted in the dormitory and the decisions of cases which are referred to Student Council shall be posted on the Student Government bulletin boards. These notices are not to be moved by unauthorized persons.

A. House Council:

1. The following shall be considered House Council offenses:

a. Failure to attend house meetings.

b. Tub or shower after 12:00 midnight.

c. Coming in late—one minute to thirty minutes..

d. Breaking own strict study hour.

e. Intentionally breaking another's strict study hour.

f. Failure to observe class groupings when taking night in town.

g. Failure to sign out and/or in.

h. Failure to ask hostess or President of Student Government for permission when there is a change of destination or when unable to return at designated hour.

i. Failure to obtain, or show, a guest card. Date not on calling list if girl has limited permission.
k. Use of telephone after 11:00 p.m.
l. Lights not out at designated time—three warnings.
m. Excessive noise—three warnings.
n. Untidy room—three warnings.
o. Smoking in unapproved place within the dormitory—three warnings.
p. Improper dress in dormitory, parlor, etc.—three warnings.

B. Student Council:

In cases involving serious infractions of rules, Student Council or Joint Council may withdraw certain privileges from students who have violated college regulations. Punishments range, according to the seriousness of the offense, from the withdrawal of the privileges concerned in minor rule infraction, to strict campusing or a modification thereof, probation, or suspension for infractions of a more serious nature. In cases of a very serious infraction, expulsion from the college will be in order.

1. Strict campus includes the following:
   a. Loses any office she may hold.
   b. May not have men callers.
   c. Must go to all meals.
   d. May not attend dances.
   e. May cut no classes.
   f. May not spend the night in a dormitory other than her own.
   g. May converse with parents only on the telephone.

h. May not be absent from the campus.

i. Will be recorded as suspended for the remainder of the session if she withdraws voluntarily from the college, except for imperative reasons.

2. Waiving of Penalties: In each case penalties may be waived by the body imposing them.

3. Exceptions and permissions:

   a. Campused students who require dental or medical treatment may leave for treatment after obtaining permission from the President of Student Government.

   b. Campused students are permitted to attend church services on Sunday mornings.

   c. Strict campus does not pertain to holidays or between semesters.

4. Notification of Parents: Parents or guardians of students who are on strict campus, placed on probation, suspended, or expelled will be notified of the causes for the withdrawal of privileges by the President of Student Council and the Dean of Women jointly.

5. A student who does not abide by her campus restrictions will be brought before Student Council and will be dealt with severely.

6. Probation:

   a. A student may be placed on social probation if it is felt necessary by Student Council or Joint Council.

   b. Any rule violated during probation will result in expulsion.

7. Immediate suspension and expulsion cases must leave campus within 24 hours after the penalty has been imposed.

CONSTITUTION
OF THE
STUDENT GOVERNMENT ASSOCIATION
MARY WASHINGTON COLLEGE

ARTICLE I.
Name
This association shall be called "The Student Government Association of Mary Washington College".

ARTICLE II.
Purpose
The purpose of this organization shall be to promote personal responsibility, loyalty, and a high sense of honor in the individual, and to represent and further the best interests of the student body and the college by inculcating the underlying principles of self-government and democracy.

ARTICLE III.
Membership
All students of Mary Washington College shall be members of this association.

ARTICLE IV.
Meetings
Section1. Regular meetings shall be held once each month. At least twenty-four hours notice shall be given.

Section 2. Special meetings shall be called by the president under the following conditions:

A. At her own discretion.

B. Upon the request of five members of the Student Council.

C. By twenty members of the student body when emergencies arise.

D. By request of the Dean of the College or the Dean of Women.

Section 3. All students are required to attend these meetings unless excused by the President of the Student Government Association.

Section 4. Quorum:

A. Two-thirds of the members of the association shall constitute a quorum.

B. A majority of those present is required for the adoption of any legislation. A majority is one more than half of those present.

ARTICLE V.

Legislative Department

The legislative power shall be vested in the Association as a whole.

ARTICLE VI.

Executive Department

Section 1. Membership:

A. President, senior.

B. Vice-President, junior or senior.

C. Secretary, junior or senior.

D. Treasurer, junior or senior.

E. House Presidents.

F. Class Representatives.

G. Town Girls' Representative.

H. Ex Officio:

1. YWCA President.

2 RA President.

3 Freshman Advisers.

Section 2. Duties:

A. Of the President:

1. To call and preside over all meetings of the Association.

2. To be responsible for the organization of the Freshman Class.

3. To act as a coordinator with all other officers and stimulate them in their duties.

4. To appoint all committees.

5. To act as chairman of the nominating committee.

6. To preside over Student Government Elections.

7. To be chairman of the handbook committee.

8. To serve on Joint Council.

B. Of the Vice-President:

1. To assume the duties of the President in her absence or at her request.

2. To act as an advisory member of House Council and organize small dormitories.

3. To act as chairman of the reviewing committee for benefits.

4. To be in charge of Loyalty Night.

5. To serve on Joint Council.

C. Of the Secretary:

1. To keep a record of all the proceedings of the Association, Student Council and Joint Council.

2. To write up cases for posting and the files.

3. To take care of all correspondence and mimeographing.

4. To make a copy of election returns. (President's vote is kept one year on file.)

5. During elections:

a. To take nominations.

b. To check grades.

c. To see that names of all candidates are approved by Joint Council.

6. To serve on Joint Council.

D. Of the Treasurer:

1. To handle efficiently the accounts of the Association.

2. To collect all money due the Association and expend the same. This is subject to the approval of the Association and under the direction of the President.

3. To serve on Joint Council.

E. Of the House Presidents:

1. To be responsible for securing a spirit of cooperation in her dormitory.

2. To cooperate with the hostess or person in charge in maintaining order and discipline.

3. To appoint a Student Government member to serve in her absence.

4. To call a regular meeting of the dormitory once a month.

5. To plan social activities of the dormitory.

6. To serve as chairman of House Council.

7. To attend any Honor Council case involving a girl from her dormitory.

F. Of the Class Representatives:

1. To represent the interest of their class on Council and be responsible for reporting to them any matters concerning them.

2. To serve as a member of the reviewing committee for Benefits.

3. To be responsible for the organization of serenades.

4. To cooperate with the officers in carrying out the business of the association.

G. Of the Town Girls' Representative:

1. To keep the day students notified of all Student Government proceedings.

2. To vote on all matters except those concerning the dormitory life of boarding students.

H. Of the Ex Officio Members:

Although these members have no voting power, they cooperate fully with the Student Council as coordinators of campus activities.

Section 3. Duties and powers of the executive department:

A. The executive power shall be vested in a Student Council which will meet once a week.

1. Special meetings may be called under the following conditions:

a. At the president's own discretion.

b. Upon the written request of two members of the Council.

c. Upon the request of ten members of the student body.

2. Student Council shall hear, decide, and affix penalties for all cases of violation of Student Government rules and regulations and standards of conduct required by the college.

3. The Student Council shall study the needs of the Association and map out a program of work for the year.

4 Student Council may refer outstanding cases of misconduct to the Joint Council for final decision. Any student may appeal by right from a decision of Student Council to the Joint Council.

Section 4. Nominations:

A. Nominations for the major offices shall be held the first week of January.

B. A committee consisting of the executive members of the Student Council and the members of the Honor Council shall prepare the slate for the four major offices of the Student Government Association; the Fire Commander; and the Honor Council President.

C. A committee consisting of the outgoing senior members of the YWCA cabinet shall prepare the slate for the five major offices of the YWCA.

D. A committee appointed by the RA president and consisting of members of the RA Council shall prepare the slate for the four major offices of the RA.

E. Additional nominations may be made:

1. From the floor at a student body meeting.

2. And by a written petition signed by 5 per cent of the student body.

F. A minimum of three nominees must be submitted for the election of those officers that are elected by the entire student body.

G. The names of nominees must be approved by Joint Council and posted for one week before elections.

H. Nominations for House Presidents are made by the present Freshman, Sophomore, and Junior Classes.

I. Nominations for class and club officers are handled by those groups.

Section 5. Elections:

A. Qualifications of Officers:

1. The Secretary of Student Government must be skilled in shorthand and typing.

2. No student may succeed herself in the same office for two succeeding years except in the case of incoming Seniors.

A. A student must have a C average based on work for the two preceding semesters, except in the case of candidates for freshman offices.

4. Ineligibility caused by conditioned grades can-

not be removed by merely making up the grades, unless the conditioned grades were due to illness or enforced absence from the college.

B. General voting procedure.

1. The entire student body shall elect the following:

a. executive members of Student Government Association, RA, and YWCA

b. the President of Honor Council and Inter-Club

c. the Fire Commander

d. the May Queen and Maid of Honor

e. Formal Dance Chairman

2. Votes which are cast by secret ballot for the major offices of SGA, YWCA, RA, and ICA, shall be counted in the presence of Student Council members. This also includes class officers, May Court, and Formal Dance Chairman.

3. Elections shall be on the basis of majority vote.

4. The count of the presidential vote must be kept on file for one year.

5. Two-thirds of the student body shall constitute a quorum for voting.

6. All elections should be completed by April 1.

C. Order of election.

1. The president of Student Government Association and the president of Honor Council (to be elected between February 1 and February 15).

2. The presidents of YWCA, RA, and ICA.

3. Vice-President, Secretary, Treasurer of Student Government Association and Fire Commander.

4. Vice-President, Secretary, Treasurer, Freshmen Commissioners of YWCA.

5. Vice-President, Secretary, and Treasurer of RA

6. Class Elections.

a. President shall have preference over all other elections.

b. Class representatives for each of the four classes. The freshman representative is to be elected immediately before Christmas.

7. There shall be a house president from the incoming Junior or Senior Class for each of the dormitories.

a. Freshman dormitories elected by the present Freshman and Sophomore Classes.

b. Sophomore dormitories elected by the present Freshman Class.

c. Junior dormitories elected by the present Sophomore Class.

d. Senior dormitories elected by the present Junior Class.

8. Club presidents shall be elected within their groups.

9. The Editors-in-Chief of the **Battlefield, Bullet, Epaulet** shall be elected within these respective organizations.

D. Further Elections.

1. May Queen—must meet the academic qualifications and come from the Senior Class. Nominations are open to the entire student body.

2. Maid of Honor—must meet the same qualifications as the May Queen.

3. May Court.

a. each class elects six representatives.

b. the Queen and her court shall elect the two flower girls and the two train bearers who may come from any class.

4. Formal Dance Chairman.

a. elected from the Junior Class in the spring preceding her Senior year.

b. must have served at least one year on the Formal Dance Committee.

Section VI. Resignation or Removal from Office.

A. The resignation of any officer may be requested by Joint Council or Student Council, provided the said person has failed to perform efficiently the duties pertaining to her office, or because of misconduct.

B. A vacancy caused by resignation or removal from office shall be filled in the same manner as previously.

C. In the extended absence of a House President, a substitute shall be nominated by the Student Council and elected by the dormitory concerned.

Section VII. Installation.

Installation exercises shall be held as soon after the fall elections as is possible, at which time the newly elected Council members shall subscribe to the following oath:

"I do hereby solemnly promise to support and maintain the Constitution of the Student Government Association of Mary Washington College and I pledge my best efforts to the efficient performance of the duties of ....of said association, to which office I have been elected."

ARTICLE VII

Judicial Department

Section 1. The judicial powers shall be vested in a Student Council and a Joint Council.

Section 2. Duties and powers of the executive department:

A. To review the nomination slate for all officers of the association.

B. To hear and decide outstanding cases of misconduct and to affix such punishment as may be necessary.

C. To hear appeals.

D. To meet in the interest of the association.

Section 3. Membership.

A. The four executive officers of the Student Council.

B. Three faculty members appointed by the Chancellor of the College, one of whom shall act as chairman of the Council.

C. The Chancellor of the college shall be an ex officio member without a vote but with the power of veto.

Section 4. Meetings.

A. At the call of the chairman.

B. At the request of any member.

ARTICLE VIII

Freshman Training

Each year the period of two weeks from the day of arrival shall be regarded as a period of training and orientation for Freshmen and all other new students in the college. No elections requiring the vote of Freshmen shall be held until October 20.

A Freshman Class sponsor is appointed by the administration for the purpose of assisting the Freshmen throughout the entire year.

ARTICLE IX

Rules and Regulations

The rules and regulations for the government of the students under the Constitution shall be formulated by the Student Council and approved by Joint Council.

ARTICLE X

Amendments

Amendments may be made to this Constitution in the following manner: Any student may propose an amendment. Such proposal shall be made in writing and submitted to the Student Council. If acted upon favorably by Student Council, the proposed amendment shall then be posted for one week, after which it shall be referred to the student body. If two-thirds of the students, provided a quorum is present, vote in favor of the proposed amendment, said amendment shall then become a part of the Constitution.

Amendment I.

Section 1. Nominees

Students nominated for president by the nominating committees of Student Government, Honor Council, Y.W.C.A., Recreation Association, or the Inter-Club Association, if chosen by two or more of the above organizations, must select the one they prefer to run for. The nominee, if she fails to succeed in winning the desired office, may drop down and run for the other presidency or presidencies for which she was nominated, as long as she was nominated by the association's committee.

Section 2. Election

The election schedule must be arranged so each association president will be elected on a different day. Elections shall be in the following sequence: president of the Student Government Association, president of the Honor Council, president of the Y.W.C.A., president of the Recreation Association, and the president of the Interclub Association.

Amendment II.

Section 1. Freshman Dormitory Personnel:

A. One house president.

B. Three freshman counselors each in Virginia and Willard dormitories. In the smaller dormitories the number will be in proportion to the number of freshmen in that dormitory as the Student Council sees necessary.

Section 2. Duties:

A. House President:

1. Represents her dormitory as a voting member on both Y.W.C.A. and Student Council.

2. Perform all other duties as set fourth in Article VI., Section 2,E.

B. Freshman Counselors:

1. Perform counseling duties.

2. Carry out dormitory regulations.

3. Aid the house president in planning dormitory activities and vesper programs.

4. Accompany any girl on her floor who is to appear before Student Council.

5. Work with the Freshman Commission on the Annual Toy Show.

6. At the end of her tenure of office submit to the hostess an evaluation or anecdotal report on each girl on her floor.

Section 3. Election:

1. Freshman dormitory house presidents and counselors will be nominated by the incoming junior class and a joint committee composed of the Y.W.C.A. nominating committee and the Student Council.

2. They will be elected by the joint committee composed of the Y.W.C.A. nominating committee and the Student Council.

INTER-CLUB ASSOCIATION

Policies

I. The Inter-Club Association of Mary Washington College is the coordinating unit of club activities and a clearing house for the discussion of the problems of the extra-curricular program for the mutual benefit of every student at Mary Washington College. As such, it shall reserve the right to exclude from membership any club or organization which does not have a stated purpose and a functioning program.

II. In order to be recognized and pursue a program on campus, a club must hold membership in the Inter-Club Association and conform to the policies and by-laws of the Inter-Club Association. For religious clubs or organizations membership in the Inter-Club Association shall be optional.

III. Application for membership in the Inter-Club Association shall be a petition stating the name of the organization, its purposes, an outline of activities planned for the school year, the name of its proposed sponsor, and proposed meeting time and place. This petition may be presented at any regular meeting of the Inter-Club Council.

IV. The Inter-Club Council collects semester reports of activities and accomplishments from each club in the Association. These reports are compared with the established purposes of the clubs as stated in their constitutions. If it is found that any club is not following its purposes to the best of its ability, then the president of Inter-Club Association, after consultation with both the Council and the president of the club in question, shall have the authority to dismiss this club from the Inter-Club Association. After probation of one semester, the dismissed club may request readmission to the Association, providing that a sincere interest in the purposes of the club, and the intention to follow them, are proven by its members. Approval for readmission of a club to the Association shall be left to the discretion of the Inter-Club Council.

Purpose

The purpose of the Inter-Club Association shall be to insure a coordinated program of club activities; to promote cooperation; and to enable each student to derive the greatest possible benefit from the extra-curricular activities at Mary Washington College.

Membership

The membership of the Inter-Club Association consists of the presidents of all of the recognized clubs and organizations at Mary Washington College. The Inter-Club Council, elected by and from Association, consists of representatives of groups of clubs having similar or related purposes.

THE INTER-CLUB ASSOCIATION
POINT SYSTEM
as revised 1955-56

I. PURPOSE OF THE POINT SYSTEM:

To help students **avoid an overload** of extracurricular responsibilities for the following reasons:
1. to prevent forced neglect of class work
2. to discourage neglect of extracurricular duties
3. to distribute offices among a greater number of people

The Inter-Club Council earnestly hopes that students will seriously consider the above reasons and use the greatest discretion in accepting offices. The present revision of the system is aimed at allowing more flexibility in the combination of offices possible for the benefit of the students in the hope that such liberty will not be abused.

II. CLASSIFICATION

Offices are classified as follows:
Absolute; Major; Secondary; and Minor.

III. DISTRIBUTION

Individuals may hold:
1 Absolute, or
1 Major and 1 Secondary, or
1 Major and 1 Minor, or
2 Secondary, or
1 Secondary and 2 Minor, or
3 Minor

This distribution is the maximum load permissible per person. In many cases, considering the nature of the offices, a student would be unwise to accept the load permitted in the above distribution. No person may hold more than one office in a particular organization.

IV. OFFICES

ABSOLUTE

Presidents of SGA, YWCA, ICA, RA, and Honor Council
Vice President of SGA
Class Presidents
Editors of student publications

MAJOR

Other officers of ICA

Except those stated elsewhere, all club or organization presidents including presidents of local honorary groups.

(NOTE: President of national honorary fraternities and Cap and Gown are exempt from the point system except when serving on the Inter-Club Council.)

BULLET news and managing editors, advertising manager

BATTLEFIELD Photography and copy editors, business and advertising managers.

Class Vice-Presidents

Formal Dance chairman

Other officers of SGA and members of Student Council

RA: Vice President, Secretary, Treasurer, Social and Publicity Chairman

YWCA: Vice President, Secretary, Treasurer, Entertainment and Publicity Chairmen

(NOTE: Freshman House Presidents, who serve equally on Student Council and YWCA Cabinet, and club presidents who serve on RA Council, will be considered as holding only one major office.)

SECONDARY

Other members of RA Council not included in the Major group

Other members of YWCA Cabinet not included in the Major group

73

MINOR

Other class, club or organization officers
Others on publications staffs
Band, Choir, and Glee Club officers
Presidents of groups representing home states or
   areas
Fire Commander

V. The names of all officers of an organization must be reported as soon as they are elected to the Inter-Club Council. All changes in office during the year must also be reported.

VI. Deliberate violation of the point system will result in appropriate disciplinary action by the Inter-Club Council.

Officers

President..Joanne Insley
Vice President..Marlene Bost
Sec.-Treas...Ruth McCulloch

Council

Athletic Clubs.......................................Madeleine Smith
Drama and Speech........................Mary Ann McDermott
Fine Arts Clubs...................................Laura Clarkson
Language Clubs....................................Barbara Pultz
Miscellaneous.......................................Nancy Foley
Publications...Judy Denton
Religious Organizations..........................Alma Rowe
Science Clubs.....................................Alice Beazley
Social Science Clubs............................Evelyn Weston
Sophomore Class Pres............................Cathy Cooper
Junior Class Pres................................Libby Foster
Senior Class Pres...............................Peggy Preston
Y.W.C.A. Representatives.......................Shirley Mauldin

74

The Inter-Club Association

ATHLETIC ORGANIZATIONS

Cavalry: Major Lo Ann Todd.

If you're the out door type and like hikes, etc., then look into the Cavalry. It is open to girls who are taking riding, also to girls who can pass a test on horsemanship.

Concert Dance: Pres. Mary Lou Fletcher.

Perfected movement to music—that's the specialty of this organization and the apprentice group which are chosen from the Junior Dance Club.

Fencing Club: Pres. Nancy Doner.

En Garde! ! Exciting and strenuous exercises await all of those who have had instruction in fencing. If you want to learn, there is room for you too in the Junior Fence Club.

Hoofprints: Pres. Mary Byrne.

Members are chosen from girls who have completed one semester of riding and who have shown an interest and ability in horsemanship.

Outing Club: Pres. Marty Brittingham.

For girls who like camping, hikes, and outdoor trips and would like to learn how to make them more fun and interesting, look into the Outing Club.

Physical Education Majors Club: Pres. Dorothy Scott.

This group is open to those interested in further knowledge of the requirements and opportunities of physical education as a profession.

75

Terrapin: Pres. Marcia Stambach.

> This is the organization for Mary Washington Mermaids. It is open to all who can pass the swimming try-outs. Their big splash of the year is the Aquacade.

DRAMA AND SPEECH ORGANIZATIONS

Alpha Psi Omega: Pres. Ginger Nettles.

> The National Honorary Dramatics Fraternity on the Hill is composed of the select few who are chosen each semester because of their outstanding endeavors in the field of drama.

Mary Washington Players: Pres. Jo Dubin.

> If you are interested in dramatic activity, join the Players group and have fun working and learning. There's a chance to help with costume, scenery, lighting and all phases of the theater.

Mike Club: Pres. Lynn Eadie.

> The Mike Club assumes the responsibility of directing and sponsoring Station WMWC. The station is organized on a non-commercial basis, but is run much the same as a professional station.

Strawberry Leaf Society: Pres. Amelia Page King.

> This organization is composed of students who work on the National Forensic Tournament held annually at Mary Washington College during Easter vacation.

Zeta Phi Eta: Pres. Mary Ann McDermott.

> This is the National Professional Speech Arts Fraternity for women. It is open to all junior and senior dramatic arts and speech majors who can meet the necessary requirements.

FINE ARTS CLUBS

Art Club: Pres. Jane Shuman.

The Art club is composed of art majors who want to carry their interest in painting, drawing, and sculpture outside the classroom.

Mu Phi Epsilon: Pres. Nancy Brogden.

This organization is the National Professional Music Sorority on the Hill, the only chapter in Virginia. To attain membership, a student must have at least a B average in her music courses, and an overall C average.

Organ Guild: Pres. Laura Clarkson.

The requirements to join this organization are that you must be taking or must have taken one year of organ. The members furnish the music for the Assembly and Convocation programs.

LANGUAGE CLUBS

Athenaeum: Pres. Patty Sue Hess.

Light into the ancient world! If you want to learn more about the classical studies, Latin and Greek, join Athenaeum, for this organization promotes both interest and appreciation in these subjects.

Eta Sigma Phi: Pres. Carolyn Six.

This organization, the National Honorary Classical Fraternity, is open to all outstanding students in Latin and Greek.

Le Cercle Francais: Pres. Susan Bender.

If you're taking Intermediate French or the more advanced courses, this is a club for you. Your pronunciation will be kept in tip-top shape, for French is spoken at all meetings.

Phi Sigma Iota: Pres: Jean Durham.

This organization, the National Honorary Romance Language fraternity will help prepare you for graduate school or other positions requiring knowledge of the romance languages. It is open to juniors and seniors with a 2.5 average in the romance languages.

El Club Hispanoamericano: Pre. Barbara Pultz.

This club is open to all of you who are interested in Spanish. You will have an opportunity to practice your Spanish, too, for it is spoken at all meetings.

MISCELLANEOUS CLUBS

Alpha Phi Sigma: Pres. Nancy Foley.

This organization is Mary Washington's answer to Phi Beta Kappa. It is open to all students who have been on the Dean's List for two consecutive semesters with a 2.30 average for 2 semesters combined.

Alumnae Daughters: Pres. Mary Montague Hudson.

This organization is for the daughters of former Mary Washington students. They coordinate activities between the Alumnae Association and the college.

Cap and Gown: Pres. Susan Bender.

Cap and Gown—a senior's dream! Open only to the

approximately twelve most outstanding seniors in leadership, scholarship, and service to the college.

Hometown Groups, not actually clubs, but social groups sponsored by the Alumnae Association, have been formed at the request of girls from various areas with the aid of the home chapter of the Alumnae Association. Thus far, three groups have been formed:

The Eastern Shore (Of Virginia) Group—
The Alexandria (Virginia) Group—
The Connecticut Group—

Town Girls: Pres. Carol Kesel.

The Town Girls Club is for non-boarding students of the Fredericksburg area. It serves to link the town girls closer to boarding students and campus activities.

PUBLICATIONS

Battlefield: Editor Foncie Lawrence.

The annual publication of the student body of Mary Washington College presents the story, through words and pictures, of your life on the Hill.

Bullet: Editor Betty Sydnor.

The Bullet comes out twice a month. It seeks to present news of the campus and other colleges in an unbiased, objective manner.

Epaulet: Editor Frances Hogue.

The Epaulet is a quarterly magazine which provides a source of publication for creative works of talented students and enables the student body to share in an appreciation of student literature and expression.

Sigma Tau Delta: Pres. Judy Denton.

This organization is the National Honorary English Fraternity. It is open to junior and senior majors who have a B average in their major, a C average in all other subjects, and have had at least 1000 words published.

RELIGIOUS ORGANIZATIONS

Baptist Student Union: Pres. Dot Carwile.

This organization serves to link the MWC Baptist students closer to the local Baptist churches. The Union also furnishes a place for worship and relaxation to all students.

Canterbury Club: Pres. Alma Rowe.

An organization of Episcopal college students meeting for work, worship, study, and fun.

Christian Science Organization: Pres. Betty Tuttle.

Christian Youth Group: Pres. Pat Treadway.

Hillel: Pres. Eleanor Goldstein.

Hillel is a national organization devoted to cultural, religious and social service among Jewish students.

Interfaith Council: Pres. Betty Tuttle.

This council is composed of the presidents of each religious group. Through this council programs are sponsored to enrich the spirit of interfaith.

Lutheran Club: Pres. Judy Townsend.

This club serves to unite Lutheran girls in a spirit of faith.

Newman Club: Pres. Gertrude Hawke.

The purpose of this club is to enable Catholic girls to deepen their spiritual feeling and to enrich their temporal lives through a balanced program of religious, intellectual, and social activities.

Wesley Foundation: Pres. Shirley Meeks.

Wesley Foundation strives to unite Methodist students on the Hill in a service for Christian living and to expand their spiritual growth.

Westminster Fellowship: Pres. Barbara Hitchings.

An organization uniting Presbyterian girls in a spirit of fellowship.

SCIENCE CLUBS

Chi Beta Phi: Pres. Alice Beazley.

This organization is the National Honorary Scientific fraternity. Membership in Chi Beta Phi is the highest honor a science major can obtain. It is open to juniors, seniors, and outstanding sophomores. Requirements include a B average in natural science and a C average in all other subjects.

Home Economics Club: Pres. Anne Lenzi.

Interested in Home Ec? You can accumulate points and gain active membership in this club by participating in its activities.

81

Mu Alpha Chi: Pres. Betty Carol Womack.

This organization is open to those majoring in medical technology, and pre-medical students.

Physical Therapy Club: Pres. Patricia O'Heir.

This organization is open to any student with an active interest in physical therapy. The club's activities include discussions, lectures, and field trips.

Pi Nu Chi: Pres. Linda Hornor.

Mary Washington's organization for you Florence Nightingales to be is Pi Nu Chi. It is open to all the pre-nursing students and has some wonderful activities including a trip to the hospital at U.Va.

Psi Chi: Pres. Vicki Majure.

This organization provides a goal for students interested in psychology, for it is the National Honorary Society in Psychology. You must have a B average or better in your psychology courses and at least a C average in all others.

Psychology Club: Pres. Beth Kindley.

If you'd really like to know more about psychology, this organization is open to all sophomores, juniors, and seniors who are interested in the field.

Science Club: Pres. Marjorie Maupin.

This organization is for all sophomore, junior, and senior science majors with a C average in science.

SOCIAL SCIENCE CLUBS

Oriental Club: Pres. Deane Ford.

This club is open to all of those who show a decided interest in learning about the Far East, its culture, people, religions, and philosophies. Membership will be extended to those who prove their willingness to devote time and interest to the club.

Pi Gamma Mu: Pres. Sally Cook.

This is the National Fraternity for social science majors. You must have a B average in social science courses and not have failed any courses to be eligible for membership.

Sigma Omega Chi: Pres. Evelyn Weston.

This is a club of sociology majors having twelve hours in sociology. Members are taken in in their junior year. Requirements include a C average.

Sigma Tau Chi: Pres. Barbara Craft.

This organization is for economics majors. Its purpose is to further interest and knowledge in economics for sophomores, juniors, and seniors who have completed six hours of economics and have a C average.

World Affairs Club: Pres. Ann Lynwood Jones.

This club has been organized to promote understanding of current and historical national and international events. Membership is open to all who show an active interest in the club's activities.

Y.W.C.A. CABINET 1956-1957

Officers:

President..Audrey Neff
Vice President..Sandy Ball
Secretary..Jean Hurt
Treasurer..Jo Markwood
Executive Secretary....................................Susan Bender

Cabinet:

Association..Leigh Goodrich
Campus Social Service.................................Ruth McCulloch
Chapel and Devotions..................................Shirley Mauldin
Community Social Service...........................Susan Hughes
Entertainment..Pat Ellis
Finance...Judy Martin
Inter-Faith Representative..........................Ruth Gray
Music...Kit Johnson
President of Senior Commission.................Jackie McDaniel
Property...Margaret Mahon
Publication..Jane Nessenthaler
Publicity...Snookie Woods
Social...
Vespers...Bunny Woodson
World Affairs..Lou Ann Harrison

House Presidents:

Willard..Peggy Kelly
Cornell..Carole Buskell
Betty Lewis...Isabel Gill

Ex Officio:

President of SGA...Emmy Hepford
President of RA..Barbara Zimmer

YOUNG WOMEN'S CHRISTIAN ASSOCIATION
Purpose
The realization that our lives, as students, are more than material, more than the pursuit of knowledge, more than the flight after personal happiness, led to the establishment of the Young Women's Christian Association of Mary Washington College. It declares its purpose to be:

"We, the members of the Young Women's Christian Association of Mary Washington College, unite in the desire to realize full and creative life through a growing knowledge of God.

We determine to have a part in making this life possible for all people.

In this task we seek to understand Jesus and follow Him."

Y.W.C.A. MEMBERSHIP
It is the privilege of every student to become a member of the Young Women's Christian Association of Mary Washington College. Membership can be attained by pledging oneself to uphold the purpose of the association. Members may be participants in a Freshman Activity Group or a committee composed of students from every class or they may be associates. Associates are those who do not actively participate in either of the above groups, but who do uphold the standards of their "Y." These associates are entitled to a vote in matters concerning the Y.W.C.A., and they are privileged to participate in the activities of the association.

Committee Work
Groups of students from all classes organized in standing committees make possible the functioning of a wide

variety of activities. Members of these committees are active in the planning and execution of the work of their committees.

FRESHMAN COMMISSION

Groups

Freshman members of the association have the same standing as upper-classmen members since they are invited to join committees the first semester. All freshmen are encouraged to participate in one of the freshman commission groups in order to learn more about the functions of the local, national, and international Y.W.C.A.'s. The work within the freshman commission group is governed by the needs of the Freshmen in the group. From each of the groups is chosen a commissioner to represent the group and a portion of the freshman class in the Freshman Commission and the Y. W. Cabinet. A traditional project of the freshman commission groups is that of making toys for underprivileged children. These toys are exhibited at a doll show in December, and they are later distributed to the children at parties. Discussions, seminars, Bible studies are held in addition to activities of a more social nature.

Y.W.C.A. Cabinet

The cabinet of the Y.W.C.A. is composed of the officers, the chairmen of the standing committees, ex officio members from Student Government, Freshman Commission, and R.A. The officers and the chairman are chosen from members of the association.

It is the purpose of the Cabinet to serve the campus by projecting a Christian philosophy into every phase of college life, by building the physical, developing the mental and social and inspiring the spiritual.

Senior Commission

The Senior Commission is **composed of capable Juniors and Seniors** who are chosen by the Y.W. Cabinet to work as senior **advisers** for the Freshman Commission and to help the Freshman Class as a whole to feel more at home on the Hill.

Freshman Commission

The Freshman Commission is chosen to represent the Freshman Class in the Y.W.C.A. It is organized in the same manner as the Y. W. Cabinet and cooperates with the Cabinet on many of its activities. One of the highest honors attainable by a freshman is to be elected a Y. W. C. A. Commissioner.

Y. W. C. A. ACTIVITIES

The Kid Party

The Kid Party, scheduled for Friday evening the **second week of the fall semester,** is anticipated with enthusiasm by students and faculty alike. Freshmen, dressed as little girls, compete for the coveted first prize and the recognition that comes with it. The "kids" parade before three judges who choose the best "kid" on the basis of childlike simplicity of dress and manner.

Peanut Week

A week before the Thanksgiving Holidays peanut shells are distributed in the dining halls. Within the shell is to be found the name of some student to whom one is secretly to play "peanut." The object of the game is for everyone to see how nice she can be to her "peanut" without the latter finding out just who is the thoughtful person. The culmination of the fun comes on the night of the "Peanut Party," when everyone learns the identity of her heretofore unknown benefactor.

87

Big and Little Sisters

The Big and Little Sister Plan is sponsored by the Y.W.C.A. and explains why you received a letter from some "nice stranger" who informed you she was your "big sister." Although you had not heretofore been cognizant of the relationship, you were assured such a one existed and were urged to write "real soon" to such and such an address.

During the summer each upperclassman desiring a "little sister" is given the name of an incoming Freshman in order that she may establish a friendship with her and help her in her preparation by answering any questions about the college that may arise. There is always a great eagerness on registration day to hunt out one's sister.

During the first few months the big sister helps her little sister to become adjusted to college life and acts as her little sister's adviser throughout the year and **sometimes throughout the remainder of her college career.**

Religious Emphasis Week

To increase the spiritual life and interest of the entire student body, "Y" sponsors Religious Emphasis Week sometime during February, bringing to the campus outstanding religious leaders to counsel and inspire.

College girls meeting together at various gatherings during this period of particular religious emphasis, whether it be in Morning Watch, in seminars, or in personal interviews, crystallize beliefs and receive fresh impetus to religious activities.

RECREATION ASSOCIATION COUNCIL
1956-1957

Officers

President..Barbara Zimmer
Vice-President.....................................Emy Villanueva
Secretary...Bonnie McCracken
Treasurer...Cindy Welsh

Chairmen

Archery...Pat Briley
Basketball..Jane Oakes
Bowling...Eula Kindley
Cabin...Pat Cain
General Sports......................................Joan Pillsbury
Golf..Phyllis Hartleb
Hockey..Pete Dallas
Publicity...Yvonne Lewis
Social..Pat Riley
Softball..Allene Tyler
Tennis..Snookie Woods
Volleyball..Carrie Lee Briscoe

Representatives

Senior..Lucile Fletcher
Junior..Harriet Ayres
Sophomore...Andy Milne
Freshman..To Be Elected

Club Presidents

Concert Dance.......................................Mary Lou Fletcher
Fencing...Nancy Doner
Hoof Prints...Mary Byrne
Outing..Marty Brittingham
Terrapin..Marcia Stambach

Miscellaneous

Bullet..Joan Essick

Ex-Officio

Student Government..................................Emmy Hepford
Y.W.C.A...Audrey Neff

The Recreation Association

The purpose of the Recreation Association shall be to promote wholesome and healthful activity, to stimulate an interest in sports, dance, and recreation, to create a spirit of good sportsmanship, and to cooperate with other campus organizations in promoting and maintaining the highest standards of college life.

The Recreation Association of Mary Washington College is a member of the national organization, The Athletic Federation of College Women. A program of sports, dance, and recreational activities to ease the strain of a busy life and to build efficiency is needed in any college. It is for such purposes that the Recreation Association offers a varied program of activities to meet the growing needs of the students.

Every student enrolled in Mary Washington College is a member of R.A. and is eligible to participate in the activities sponsored by it. Early in the fall a sign-up day is held at which time every student is given an opportunity to join a committee to help in planning and carrying out its activities.

The Recreation Association conducts an orientation program for freshmen early in the fall semester to describe the activities and functions of the organization.

Sports

During the fall the college sports program includes intramural hockey, bowling, golf, archery, tennis and basketball tournaments. The Terrapin Club gives an exhibition and the Hoof Prints has a gymkhana.

Bowling and volleyball begin in January and February along with the general sports activities.

The spring features archery, golf, tennis, softball, riding, and the continuation of the volleyball tournament. The Terrapin Club holds its annual aquacade and the Hoof Prints Club sponsors its annual horse show.

All students are eligible for teams, and are urged to watch the Recreation Association bulletin board in the Student Activity Building and to listen for other announcements of practice hours and game schedules.

The riding, swimming, fencing, outing, and modern dance clubs—major clubs in the association—sponsor numerous activities throughout the school year and offer many opportunities for students to participate in the college sports, dance, and recreational programs.

Devil-Goat Rivalry

"And the Goat shall be your emblem." The Goat is a symbol of which you shall grow to be proud.

Devil-Goat rivalry prevails throughout the year, and is evidenced in several sports events. The climax of the competition is attained on Devil-Goat Day, when the Devils and Goats meet in a final series of events to determine the victor in the year's struggle. Students who enter the college in an odd year are termed Devils, and those who enter in an even year are named Goats. There is a rivalry between the two clans each trying to amass the greater total number of points in frequent contests during the college session. At the end of the year the team having won the greater number of points is suitably rewarded.

The Cabin

Upon the crest of a high hill, in a remote and secluded section of the campus, stands the "Cabin," which can boast of electric lights, running water, and a large indoor as well as outdoor fireplace, all of which help in creating a rustic atmosphere.

Linen, china, and cutlery are furnished by the college for any group of students wishing to go to the cabin for picnic suppers or parties. Reservations must be made with the Cabin Chairman and arrangements made for a member of the faculty to accompany the group as chaperon. A member of the cabin committee must also accompany the group.

Because of the location of the cabin surrounded by woods and leaves, great caution must be exercised when fires are built out-of-doors. Outdoor fires must be limited to days and periods when they do not constitute a hazard. They should never be built during dry weather and on windy days and must at all times be in compliance with the State law.

Alumnae Association

Mary Washington College has a large and active Alumnae Association with members scattered over the United States and foreign countries. Many of the alumnae have achieved distinction in the fields of Art, Music, Literature, Business, Social Work, Education, and Politics.

The purpose of the Association is to continue the ties between former students and campus life, to promote good fellowship among the members, to interchange ideas on alumnae and educational problems, to establish and promote chapters of the Association, and to aid in very possible way Mary Washington College of the University of Virginia. The Association endeavors to keep all former students in touch with news from the college.

The alumnae office is in Room 204 of Ann Carter Lee Hall, where the Executive Secretary is located.

Some of the activities of the Alumnae Association are publishing four news bulletins a year, keeping records of all former graduates and students of the college, and organizing new chapters to become active with the present twenty alumnae chapters. The highlight of each year is the annual Homecoming held the first weekend in April at the college. A list of alumnae is available by geographical locations.

Membership in the Association does not require a degree but it is for everyone who has established credit at the college.

CHURCH DIRECTORY

The churches in Fredericksburg represent practically every denomination, and all extend a cordial welcome to the students. While church attendance is not compulsory, all students are encouraged to affiliate themselves with some church during their residence here. The spirit of cooperation between the college and the various local churches is one of mutual helpfulness.

Catholic	Rev. James J. Widmer
Christian	Rev. Hunter H. Newman
Christian Science	
Fairview Baptist	Rev. David Ray Hepler
Fredericksburg Baptist	Dr. Robert F. Caverlee
Reformed Jewish Temple	Rabbi Isadore Franzblau
Lutheran	Rev. William Leigh Bell
Methodist	Rev. James W. Smith, Jr.
Presbyterian	Rev. Samuel L. Belk
St. George's Episcopal	Rev. T. G. Faulkner, Jr.
Trinity Episcopal	Rev. Harry Rains
Zoan Baptist	Rev. H. Morgan, Jr.

PLACES OF HISTORIC INTEREST IN FREDERICKSBURG

Near the College

Ferry Farm, the boyhood home of George Washington.

Home and monument of George Washington's mother, Mary Washington.

Masonic Lodge, where George Washington was made a Mason.

"Kenmore," home of Betty Washington Lewis.

Home of Matthew Fontaine Maury.

Home of John Paul Jones.

"Chatham."

The first apothecary shop in America.

James Monroe's Law Office.

Old Salem Church.

Rising Sun Tavern.

National Cemetery.

Confederate Cemetery.

Old Slave Block.

INDEX

96

MARY WASHINGTON MARCHING SONG

Let's raise a cheer for Mary Washington,
    You know we'll love her 'til we die—
The happy hours in our college,
    Friendship and knowledge—
We'll hold her standards high,
    And when we leave dear Mary Washington
Still all the world shall hear us say,
    We're mighty proud of Alma Mater—
    M.W.C. of U. Va.

CPSIA information can be obtained
at www.ICGtesting.com
Printed in the USA
BVHW050943060223
657963BV00009B/655